D0530380

Islam
in words and pictures

Sarah Thorley
Designed and illustrated by the author

CONTENTS

WORD LIST

Islam a religion; the word means to 'submit' to God, to obey God
Muslims the people who follow the religion of Islam
Muhammad the great leader and prophet (see below) of Islam
the Qur'an the holy book of Islam
mosque the building where Muslims meet to worship
Arabic the language Arab people speak; the Qur'an is written in Arabic
Allah the Arabic word for God
Mecca the holiest city of Muslims; it is in Arabia
the Hajj the great pilgrimage (journey to a holy place) to Mecca
Eid the word means 'festival'; there are two great Eids each year
Zakat the money that Muslims must give away for charity
Ramadan the month when Muslims fast (see below)
Hijra the name given to the journey that Muhammad made from Mecca to Medina
madrasah the classes Muslim children go to after school to study the Qur'an
Imam a Muslim teacher and leader of prayer

to fast to go without food or drink for a certain time for religious reasons
prophet holy person who is sent by God to tell his will, a messenger of God's word
shrine place containing a very holy object
to sacrifice to kill an animal and offer it to God
pilgrim person who makes a journey to a holy place

Dates c.e. stands for Christian or Common Era (the years since the birth of Jesus).
For Muslim dates, see p. 25.

08 JUN 2022

WITHDRAWN

York St. John College

3 8025 00492735 9

1 Beliefs

There are Muslims in countries all over the world, but they all believe in the same FIVE PILLARS OF ISLAM. Every Muslim must try to carry out these five duties. They make a difference to everyday life and to everything a Muslim does.

1. ABOUT GOD

A Muslim believes that 'There is only one God and Muhammad is his prophet' (or messenger).
Here is a photograph of the doorway of a mosque in Africa. Can you read the writing in English?
The writing underneath is Arabic.

2. PRAYER

Look at the picture of the street, on the right. Wherever Muslims happen to be, they should pray five times each day: in the early morning, at about midday, in mid-afternoon, at dusk and before going to bed. In this way they remember God all through the day.

3. MONEY

Zakat is the name for the money that Muslims must give away each year. They must give at least 2½ per cent of the value of their property and possessions. The money is used for the poor and for the welfare of the community.

The photograph on the right shows men collecting zakat outside a Birmingham mosque. It is the festival of Eid al-Fitr (see p. 20).

Here is a photograph of a zakat box at the entrance to a mosque in London. Muslims may also give money freely to charity each week.

4.   FASTING

Muslims must fast during the month of Ramadan each year. They may not eat or drink between dawn and sunset. In the drawing below a group of people are looking out for the new moon at the end of Ramadan. When they see it they will spread the news and the month of fasting will be over.

5.   THE HAJJ

All Muslims should try to make a pilgrimage to Mecca once in their lifetime. This photograph shows pilgrims at the Ka'aba, the holy building in the courtyard of the mosque in Mecca.

1. Look at the photograph taken in Africa. What does the writing over the mosque door say?
2. Who was Muḥammad?
3. How often should a Muslim pray?
4. Look at the photograph of the two men praying. Where are they? What time of day do you think it is?
5. What is zakat?
6. What is the boy doing outside the Birmingham mosque?
7. (a) What does 'to fast' mean? (b) What happens in the month of Ramadan?
8. What is the fifth duty? Look closely at the picture of Mecca and describe what you see.
9. Which of these duties do think would be the hardest to keep if you were a Muslim living in England? Why?
10. Copy one of the pictures and write a sentence about it.

2 Muhammad

In 570 C.E. a boy was born in the big trading centre of Mecca in Arabia.
His name was Muhammad. He was to become a great leader. He gave people the message of Islam with its belief in one God.
His father died before he was born and his mother died when he was six, so his grandfather and his uncle took care of him. As a boy he looked after sheep. When he grew up he worked on the trade routes helping with the camel caravans.
The picture below shows a caravan of traders arriving at a safe place for the night. Later he married his employer, a rich woman called Khadija. They had six children, but Muhammad's only descendants were through one daughter called Fatima. The others either died when they were young or their children died.

Arabia

Muhammad was upset by the way many people behaved. They lived bad lives, drinking alcohol and fighting one another. They worshipped many different idols. Muhammad began to spend a lot of time alone in the mountains thinking about these things. He began to have dreams and visions. Muslims believe that he heard the words of God, spoken by the Angel Gabriel. Muhammad himself could not read or write, but he told others what he had heard and the words were later written down. They became the Qur'an (the Muslims' Holy Book).

This is a drawing of the cave on Mount Hira where Muhammad often spent many days praying and thinking about what God wanted him to do. Today the cave is visited by pilgrims.

Muhammad began to preach Islam to the people. He said, 'Stop worshipping all these idols. There is only *one* God.' But the people of Mecca would not listen to him. They tried to kill him. When he was invited to another town called Medina, he left Mecca. There is a story about that journey to Medina. His enemies were chasing him so he hid in a cave. A spider spun a web over the mouth of the cave and a bird built a nest in a bush in front of the cave, so his enemies did not think of looking for him in there. Muslims believe that God protected him.

Muhammad's journey from Mecca to Medina is a very important event for Muslims. It is called the Hijra and Muslims count their years from that date (in the same way that Christians count their years from the time that Christ was born). The Muslim calender is explained on p. 25.

In Medina, Muhammad was welcomed and he had the first mosque built so that people could go there to worship God. He taught that people should follow God's law. He said they should love each other as equals and be kind and truthful and help those in

need. His message became popular and in the end even the people of Mecca believed him and accepted Islam. After that Islam spread quickly to many other countries.

You will notice that there are no pictures of Muhammad in this book. Muslims never draw pictures of Muhammad. They do not worship Muhammad. He is respected and honoured as the Prophet of God. Many Muslims use the words 'Blessings and peace be upon him' each time his name is spoken or written.

Muhammed died when he was sixty-three. He was buried in Medina and a mosque was later built around his tomb. It is shown in the photograph below.

1. (a) How many years ago was Muhammad born? (b) Where was he born?
2. What did many of his countrymen do that upset him?
3. Whose words did Muhammad hear in the cave on Mount Hira?
4. What happened to those words he heard?
5. Write down the story telling how God protected Muhammad on his way to Medina.
6. (a) Why did Muhammad leave Mecca? (b) What does the Hijra mean to Muslims?
7. What did Muhammad teach the people?
8. Medina is a very holy city to Muslims. Why do you think this is so?
9. Why are there no pictures of Muhammad in this book?
10. Draw a picture of a camel caravan. (The illustrations on p. 4 and p. 12 may help you.)

YORK
RE
CENTRE

3 The Qur'an

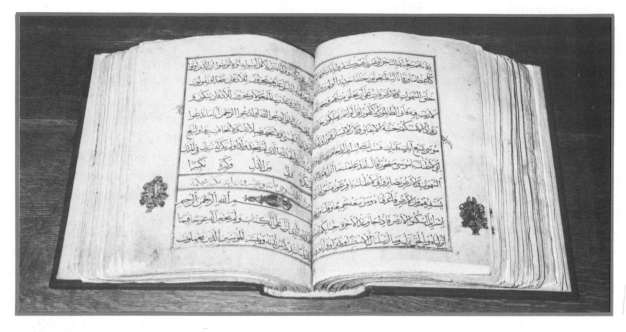

THE QUR'AN is the holy book of the Muslims. They believe it contains the words of God. The Angel Gabriel spoke these words to Muhammad between the years 610 and 632 C.E. Muhammad learnt them by heart and they were later written down in the Arabic language. The words in every copy of the Qur'an are the same. Most Muslims can read Arabic and they are all able to recite by heart from the Qur'an.

The picture above shows a copy of the Qur'an.
The writing is in Arabic; it is read from right to left.

This photograph was taken at a mosque in Iran. The man is reading the Qur'an, which rests on a wooden stand. You might see a stand like this in a Muslim home.

THE HADITH The other important books for Muslims are called the Hadith. They are reports of what Muhammad said and did. They are still used by Muslim leaders today to advise people. If someone has a problem about his faith or about business, money, family or legal matters, he would look in the Hadith to find what Muhammad said or did in such a case.

WHAT DOES THE QUR'AN SAY?

The Qur'an teaches that everything that exists belongs to God and that people are caretakers of God's world. It praises God and gives rules for life.
Chapters in the Qur'an are called suras. Every sura begins 'In the name of Allah, the Merciful and Forgiving', to show that what follows are God's words.

ABOUT GOD the Qur'an says: 'Allah has power over all things. . . . Allah hears all and knows all. . . .'
'Allah knows a man before he is born and is closer to him than his jugular vein.'

ABOUT TRUE BELIEVERS the Qur'an says: 'Share your goods with those in need . . . pray . . . keep your promises . . . stay true to God in times of difficulty. . . .'

ABOUT CHRISTIANS AND JEWS the Qur'an says they are 'People of the Book'. (The Book is the Bible.)
Muslims accept Abraham, Moses and Jesus as prophets of God. They believe that Muhammad was the greatest and last prophet. They do not believe that Jesus was the son of God. The Qur'an says: 'Allah gave to Jesus, son of Mary, signs and the power of the Holy Spirit.'

Here you can see some Muslim children in Birmingham. They come to 'madrasah' after school or at the weekend to study the Qur'an and to learn to recite it in Arabic.

1. In what language is the Qur'an written?
2. How did it come to be written?
3. What are the Hadith about?
4. Why are the Hadith still useful today?
5. What does the Qur'an teach?
6. (a) How should true Muslims act? (b) In what ways should they act as caretakers of God's world?
7. Write down two things the Qur'an says about Jesus.
8. Imagine you are describing the photographs on this page to a blind person. Comment on the rooms, the activities, boys and girls, clothes etc.
9. What do you think about children doing this sort of work after school?

4 Mosques

This picture shows a beautiful old mosque in Iran. A mosque is
a building where Muslims meet to worship God. The 'round'
roof is called a dome. The tall towers are called minarets.
From a minaret, Muslims are called to prayer five times a day
by a man known as a muezzin.

Below is the courtyard of another mosque in Iran. In hot
countries people pray outside in the courtyard. If they need to,
they can take shelter from the sun or the rain under the
archways around the courtyard. Look closely at the picture: can
you see a man and a boy washing themselves in the pool of
water before they pray?

These men are arriving at a
modern mosque in London.
Can you see a row of shoes
at the back? Everyone has to
take off their shoes when
they enter, to keep the
mosque clean for prayer.

You will see no pictures or statues in a mosque, only colourful patterns and writing from the Qur'an. There are no seats. Muslims worship on rugs on the floor. This is a picture of a mosque in India. The alcove set in the wall marks the direction of Mecca; it is called a mihrab. Muslims must always face towards Mecca when they pray. The flight of steps is called a minbar. The Imam (religious leader) speaks from the top of the steps. An Imam is not usually paid for the religious work he does. He may earn money as caretaker or secretary of a mosque or he may have another job outside the mosque.

Friday is the holy day of the week for Muslims.
Men should go to the mosque every Friday for worship. Women are not expected to go so often. During the service the Imam leads the people in prayer, he preaches to them about God and chapters from the Qur'an are read.

On other days of the week the mosque will be used for daily prayers and for teaching children about their religion. Muslims can also go there for advice about any problems in their daily lives.

1. Why is there often a fountain or a pool of water in a mosque courtyard?
2. What is the first thing Muslims do as they enter a mosque?
3. There are no pictures or statues in a mosque. How are mosques decorated?
4. Which direction must Muslims face when they pray? How can they tell where this is?
5. What happens every Friday at the mosque?
6. What does an Imam do?
7. What else is a mosque used for, besides worship?
8. Have you seen a mosque in Britain? If so, where is it? What does it look like?
9. Write down some of the ways in which a mosque is different from a church.
10. Copy the drawing above and add the right words at the end of each pointer.

5 Prayer

In a Muslim city you would hear the 'call to prayer' five times each day. The muezzin (the caller) goes up into the minaret of the mosque. (Nowadays, loudspeakers are often used to save him the climb!) This is what he calls out :
Alla-hu Akbar, Alla-hu Akbar.
Ash-hadu an la-ilaha Illal-lah.
Ash-hadu Anna Muhammadan Rasoo-lul-lah.
Hay-ye Alas-salaah.
Hay-ye Alal-falaah.

Each line is called out twice. This is what it means:
God is most great, God is most great.
I bear witness that there is only one God.
I bear witness that Muhammad is the messenger of God.
Come to prayer. Come to success.

Muslims should pray five times every day, wherever they may be. They may be in their own home or at work . . .

they may be in a beautiful mosque with fine carpets . . .

or they may go to a simple house mosque like this one. (A house with one or more rooms set aside for prayer.)

The prayers follow a set pattern and every Muslim learns them by heart. These drawings show the usual positions that Muslims should use when they pray. Muslims also say their own private prayers at any time.

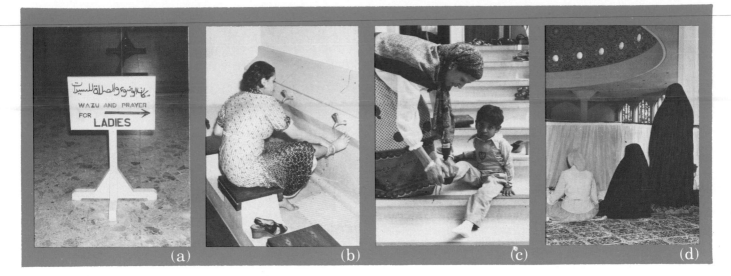

(a)   (b)   (c)   (d)

Women pray apart from the men. At the Central London mosque, where these photographs were taken, there is a separate prayer gallery and wash room for women. Before they pray, Muslims must always wash themselves. They must wash their hands, arms, face, nose and feet. (Wazu means to wash for prayer.)

You may see a Muslim carrying a string of prayer beads. There are 99 beads (or 33, used three times). In the Qur'an there are 99 names for God, e.g. the Wise, the Merciful, the Good. Muslims can say each of the names, moving their fingers along the beads as they pray. Muslims often have their own prayer rug, like the one on the left. They stand, bow or kneel on it as they pray.

Remember that whenever Muslims pray they must face towards Mecca. Some Muslims carry a compass like the one above. With the compass is a small leaflet which shows how to set it so that wherever you may be the compass will point in the direction of Mecca.

1. How often should a Muslim pray?
2. Look at the drawing of the muezzin and describe what he is doing.
3. (a) Copy out the Arabic call to prayer. (b) What does the first line mean in English?
4. Muslims bear witness to (say they believe) two things in their prayers. What are they?
5. What must Muslims remember to do before they start to pray?
6. (a) What are prayer beads for? (b) Why would a Muslim carry a compass?
7. Make up a caption for each of the small pictures at the top of this page, (a), (b), (c) and (d).
8. Write a paragraph to say why a Muslim living in Britain might have difficulty in carrying out the prayer duties. Look at each picture as you think about it.
9. Draw *either* three of the prayer positions Muslims should use *or* the three 'aids to prayer' they might have.

6 Arabia

Arabia is the country from which Islam spread.
The people who live in Arabia are called Arabs.
Muhammad was an Arab. He was born in the large trading city of Mecca in 570 C.E.

Arabia is a hot dry land. Much of it is desert.
To the west is Africa and to the east are Iran and India. People from Africa wanted to trade with people from India, so they loaded their camels and donkeys and made long journeys across the deserts of Arabia and Iran. These camel trains were called 'caravans'. At one time, Muhammad helped to organize the trade routes. Often he would travel with the camel caravans. In this way he visited many cities.

Most of the Arabs were nomads. They lived in tents and moved from place to place to find grazing for their animals. They ate a lot of dates and they could drink the camels' and goats' milk. They were fierce and cruel to their enemies, but they would share everything with their own tribe.

These days most Arabs have settled down in one place. However, some are still nomads.
The tribe in this picture has camped by a well.

This is a photograph of a very old caravanserai in the desert. It was a kind of inn where travellers could stay in safety overnight. Even the animals would be safe in the big courtyard, once the great door was closed for the night.

In Muhammad's time, Mecca was already a holy city for the Arabs. They worshipped many gods, but some believed that there was one great god who ruled over all the smaller gods and spirits. The shrine (holy place) called the Ka'aba was important even then (see p. 10).
Every Muslim tries to go there once in his or her life, even if they live thousands of miles away.
The first photograph of Mecca was taken in 1882. Here is a copy of it.

Today Arabia is called Saudi Arabia. Islam is still the Arabs' religion and their way of life. They keep many of their old customs but these two photographs show how modern much of the country is now.
One is of machinery for taking out salt from sea water. The other shows broadcasting technicians in the capital city, Riyadh.

1. What kind of country is Arabia?
2. Why did people make long journeys with their camels?
3. (a) What nationality was Muhammad? (b) Why did he travel a lot?
4. How did the nomads live?
5. What is a caravanserai?
6. Write two sentences about Mecca.
7. Muslims must face Mecca when they pray. Would Muslims living in Britain turn towards the east or the west?
8. Imagine you are an Arab trader living in about 550 C.E. Describe your journey to Iran with your goods. What did you see? What adventures did you have? Who did you meet? Illustrate your work.

7 Islam spreads

Muhammad died in 632 C.E. The leaders who came after him were called Caliphs. They were leaders of both the faith and the state. In Islam, religion and government should not be separate.

The Qur'an tells Muslims to spread the faith, so Arab armies invaded countries to the north, east and west and captured many important cities. These invasions were called jihads (holy wars). The soldiers went 'in the name of Allah'.

Most Muslims are 'Sunni' Muslims. About 12% of Muslims are 'Shi'a' Muslims. (Most Muslims in Iran, for example, are Shi'as.) The Shi'as believe that Muhammad's descendants continued to have God's guidance and they regard their lives and teachings as sacred. They commemorate the births and deaths of these 'Imams' (as they call them) and make pilgrimages to their tombs. The two most famous tombs are Ali's tomb at Najaf and Husayn's tomb at Karbala, both in Iraq. In most other respects, the Shi'as practise Islam in the same way as the Sunnis.

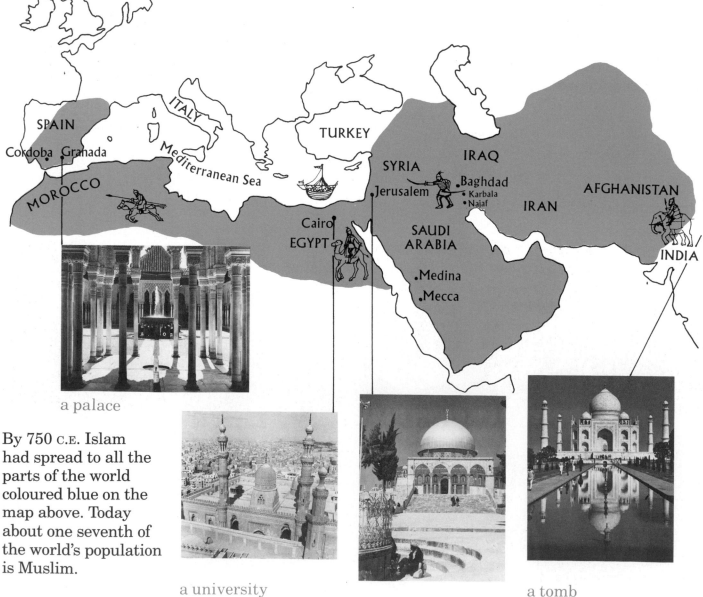

a palace

a university

a mosque

a tomb

By 750 C.E. Islam had spread to all the parts of the world coloured blue on the map above. Today about one seventh of the world's population is Muslim.

This picture, painted on tiles, is part of a fountain in a town in Iran. It shows one of Muhammad's descendants ready to go into battle.

Muslims have strict rules about war. The Qur'an says that no women, children or old people must ever be killed in war. Nor may soldiers burn crops or loot or steal. Nobody should be forced to change their religion to Islam. (Although sometimes that did happen.) In some of the countries the Muslims occupied, the people were glad to see them because their own rulers were very cruel.

Many of the Arab Muslims who settled in foreign lands were wise and learned. Some were fine craftsmen and architects (the buildings on p.14 are very famous). In three of the conquered cities universities were set up: Córdoba, Cairo and Baghdad. People came from all over Europe to learn from the Muslims. They knew more about mathematics, science, astronomy, medicine and languages than anyone else in the world at that time. Here are two examples:

Number symbols today are called Arabic numbers. Before western countries learned them from the Arabs they used Roman numbers:

ARABIC	1	2	3	4	5	6	7	8	9	10
ROMAN	I	II	III	IV	V	VI	VII	VIII	IX	X

The Arabs also invented the use of zero (0), which makes it much easier to work out sums.

$$\begin{array}{rr} \text{IV} & 4 \\ +\text{XXXX} & +40 \\ \hline \text{XXXXIV} & 44 \end{array}$$

Look at this example of the same sum in Roman and in Arabic numbers.

This is an astrolabe, an instrument which enables people to navigate by the stars. It was invented by Muslim scientists in the fourteenth century. It was a very important discovery for sailors and for people in hot countries, who usually travelled by night.

All these people were seen visiting the Central London mosque during one day.

1. What did a Caliph do?
2. Name six countries the Muslims occupied by 750 C.E.
3. Look at the map. How did the Arabs travel?
4. Write down one of the rules of war from the Qur'an.
5. Name some of the skills the Muslim invaders took with them.
6. Copy out and complete the following sum, then write it out in Roman numbers. 10+30+3=
7. Why was an astrolabe such an important invention?
8. Look at the people in the photograph above. Write down which country you think each one comes from.
9. Draw a picture of the Muslim soldier ready for battle.

8 The Hajj

Pilgrims arrive by ship at the port of Jeddah. Notice how they are dressed.

From here they are taken by bus to Mecca which is 72 km away. The umbrellas are to protect the pilgrims from the hot sun.

Hajj means pilgrimage. The people who go on a pilgrimage are called Hajji (pilgrims). Once every year, the city of Mecca is filled with thousands of Muslim pilgrims. Every Muslim tries to visit Mecca once in his or her life because it is one of the five duties of Islam. Mecca is the most holy city of Islam. If you are not a Muslim, you cannot go to Mecca.

Before they reach Mecca every pilgrim puts on a simple white robe. It shows that all people are equal before God.

The pilgrimage takes about four days. On these two pages you can follow the pilgrims' route and see the things they will do. Follow the blue arrows.

72km

This is the great mosque at Mecca. In the courtyard is the Ka'aba. It is covered with the Kiswah, a black cloth which has been embroidered in gold thread. In one corner of the Ka'aba is the Black Stone, which is said to be a meteorite which fell from heaven. Also in the courtyard is a sacred stone on which the prophet Abraham is believed to have stood. Every pilgrim goes seven times round the Ka'aba and may touch or kiss the Black Stone.

A pilgrim kisses the Black Stone

These men are working on the Kiswah. They make a new one every year!

MECCA

16

Medina is the second holiest city. Muhammad spent much of his life there. Many pilgrims visit his tomb in the Mosque.

MEDINA
482km

MINA

Before the pilgrims return home they sacrifice a lamb in memory of Abraham. They give away part of the meat to the poor (see p. 21).

Mina is a small village about eight km from Mecca. At Mina are three stone pillars which are symbols of the Devil. The pilgrims throw stones at the pillars.

These pilgrims are running backwards and forwards along a hallway between two small hills. They do it in memory of Hagar searching for water in the desert. You can read the story in the Bible (Genesis Chapter 21, verses 9–21).

The Mount of Mercy is a small hill where Muhammad gave a famous sermon. Many pilgrims climb the hill.

ARAFAT

This is the Plain of Arafat, all around Mecca. Many of the pilgrims camp out here. There are thousands of tents.

Note You will need a Bible and an atlas.
1. (a) What does Hajj mean? (b) Would *you* be able to go on the Hajj?
2. (a) What kind of clothes do Muslims wear on the Hajj? (b) Why?
3. Describe how Muslim pilgrims get to Mecca.
4. Write down what you see in the picture of the Ka'aba *or* copy out Sura 2, verses 125–7 from the Qur'an.
5. (a) What is the Black Stone? (b) What is the Kiswah?
6. (a) What do pilgrims do at Mina? (b) Why do you think they do this?
7. Read about Hagar in the Bible. Write down the story in your own words.
8. Why do many pilgrims go to Medina?
9. Look at an atlas and draw a map of Arabia. Mark on the map the places named in this chapter.

9 Food and fasting

Muslims have strict rules about what they may eat and drink.

They are not allowed to drink alcohol. It is 'haraam', which means forbidden.
The Qur'an says, 'The Devil wants only to make hatred between you, by means of alcohol and gambling, and keep you back from Allah.'

Muslims are forbidden to eat pig meat of any kind. They buy meat from their own butchers whenever they can. This is because animals must be killed in a certain way to drain the blood from the meat. The butcher says the prayer 'Allah Akbar' (God is great) three times over the animal before he kills it. The animal's throat is then cut to cause a quick death. The blood drains out and the meat is then called 'halal', which means allowed. The Qur'an says that Muslims should eat only the meat of animals which have been killed in this way.

The two photographs on this page show the outside and the inside of a Muslim butcher's shop in Birmingham.

Ramadan is the ninth month in the Islamic calender. It is a very important month for Muslims because it is the month when they fast. (Fasting means not eating for a period of time.) For 29 or 30 days Muslims do not eat or drink during the hours of daylight. This is one of the 'Five Pillars of Islam' (see p. 3). The fast starts from the moment the new moon is seen at the beginning of the month; it finishes when the new moon is seen again at the beginning of the next month.
Of course there is great excitement then and Eid al-Fitr is celebrated the next day.

Why do Muslims fast during Ramadan? There are several reasons.
First, it is the command of God in the Qur'an. Ramadan was the month when Muhammad first heard the words of God, which were later written down as the Qur'an. So, during Ramadan, Muslims remember especially to thank God for his gift of the Qur'an.
Another reason is that it teaches self-control. It can be hard to go without a drink on a hot day! It is also a reminder of what it is like to be poor and hungry and of the sufferings of the people in the world who do not have enough to eat.
Old and sick people, young children and pregnant women do not have to fast. Travellers may keep the fast later.

The picture above shows 'Al-Musaharati', the drum beaters in Egypt who wake up the people during the night to eat their last meal before dawn. In many Muslim countries, a gun is fired at dawn. Muhammad said eating should stop as soon as it is light enough to tell a black thread from a white one.

This is a timetable for Muslims living in different cities in England. It is a guide to tell them what time they should begin and end their fast each day. (Of course the dates change each year according to the new moon.)

Ramadan	October-November	London		Birmingham		Sheffield		Manchester		Leeds		Liverpool	
		Fast Begins	Ends	Fast Begins	Ends	Fast Begins	Ends	Fast Begins	Ends	Fast Begins	Ends	Fast Begins	Ends
1	Oct. 31	6.34	5.36	6.41	5.40	6.41	5.36	6.43	5.39	6.41	5.35	6.46	5.42
2	Nov 1	6.35	5.34	6.43	5.38	6.42	5.34	6.45	5.37	6.43	5.33	6.48	5.40
3	2	6.37	5.32	6.44	5.36	6.44	5.32	6.47	5.35	6.45	5.31	6.49	5.38
4	3	6.38	5.31	6.46	5.35	6.46	5.30	6.49	5.33	6.46	5.29	6.51	5.36
5	4	6.40	5.29	6.48	5.33	6.48	5.28	6.50	5.31	6.48	5.28	6.53	5.34
6	5	6.42	5.27	6.49	5.31	6.49	5.27	6.52	5.29	6.50	5.26	6.55	5.32
7	6	6.43	5.26	6.51	5.29	6.51	5.25	6.54	5.28	6.51	5.24	6.56	5.31
8	7	6.45	5.24	6.53	5.28	6.53	5.23	6.55	5.26	6.53	5.22	6.58	5.29
9	8	6.46	5.22	6.54	5.26	6.54	5.21	6.57	5.24	6.55	5.20	7.00	5.27
10	9	6.48	5.21	6.56	5.24	6.56	5.19	6.59	5.22	6.57	5.19	7.01	5.25
11	10	6.49	5.19	6.57	5.23	6.58	5.18	7.00	5.21	6.58	5.17	7.03	5.24
12	11	6.51	5.18	6.59	5.21	6.59	5.16	7.02	5.19	7.00	5.15	7.05	5.22
13	12	6.52	5.16	7.01	5.19	7.01	5.15	7.04	5.17	7.02	5.13	7.06	5.20
14	13	6.54	5.15	7.02	5.18	7.03	5.13	7.05	5.16	7.03	5.12	7.08	5.19
15	14	6.56	5.13	7.04	5.16	7.04	5.11	7.07	5.14	7.05	5.10	7.10	5.17
16	15	6.57	5.12	7.05	5.15	7.06	5.10	7.09	5.13	7.07	5.09	7.11	5.16
17	16	6.59	5.11	7.07	5.14	7.07	5.09	7.10	5.11	7.08	5.07	7.13	5.14
18	17	7.00	5.09	7.08	5.12	7.09	5.07	7.12	5.10	7.10	5.06	7.14	5.13
19	18	7.01	5.08	7.10	5.11	7.11	5.06	7.13	5.08	7.11	5.04	7.16	5.11
20	19	7.03	5.07	7.11	5.10	7.12	5.04	7.15	5.07	7.13	5.03	7.17	5.10
21	20	7.04	5.06	7.13	5.08	7.14	5.03	7.16	5.06	7.14	5.02	7.19	5.09
22	21	7.06	5.05	7.14	5.07	7.15	5.02	7.18	5.05	7.16	5.00	7.21	5.08
23	22	7.07	5.04	7.16	5.06	7.17	5.01	7.20	5.03	7.18	4.59	7.22	5.06
24	23	7.09	5.02	7.17	5.05	7.18	4.59	7.21	5.02	7.19	4.58	7.23	5.05
25	24	7.10	5.01	7.19	5.04	7.19	4.58	7.22	5.01	7.20	4.57	7.25	5.04
26	25	7.11	5.01	7.20	5.03	7.21	4.57	7.24	5.00	7.22	4.56	7.26	5.03
27	26	7.13	5.00	7.21	5.02	7.22	4.56	7.25	4.59	7.23	4.55	7.28	5.02
28	27	7.14	4.59	7.23	5.01	7.24	4.55	7.27	4.58	7.25	4.54	7.29	5.01
29	28	7.15	4.58	7.24	5.00	7.25	4.54	7.28	4.57	7.26	4.53	7.30	5.00
30	29	7.16	4.59	7.25	4.59	7.26	4.53	7.29	4.56	7.27	4.52	7.32	4.59

1. (a) What does 'haraam' mean? (b) What does 'halal' mean?
2. Look at the photograph of the shop. How can you tell it is a Muslim butcher?
3. Why do Muslims buy meat from their own butchers?
4. If you had Muslim visitors, what would you give them for dinner?
5. What is Ramadan?
6. What decides when the fast begins and ends?
7. Write down two reasons why Muslims fast.
8. Look at the timetable. At what time does the fast begin and end on 9 November in Leeds?
9. Who are 'Al-Musaharati'?
10. Draw one of the pictures and write a sentence about it.

10 Festivals

There are two main religious festivals each year which are holidays for Muslims. They are called 'Eid', which means festival. There are also some other smaller festivals.

Eid al-Fitr is the festival of 'breaking the fast'. It takes place at the end of Ramadan (the month during which Muslims fast). At Eid al-Fitr Muslims give money to the poor (see p. 2).

(see p. 2)

They buy new clothes and eat a special meal. They send cards to their friends and give presents to one another. But the day always starts with prayers at the mosque.

These three photographs were taken outside the mosque in Birmingham on Eid morning. Here, men are queuing up to go into the mosque to pray.

This family are dressed up in their new clothes.

Here are some boys buying hats to cover their heads before they pray.

On the right is a mosque in Egypt which has been decorated with lights especially for Eid.

20

Eid al-Adha, the festival of sacrifice, is the other big festival. This takes place each year at the end of the Hajj. All over the world Muslims give thanks for those who have been on the great pilgrimage. After visiting the mosque to pray, it is the custom for every family that can afford it to sacrifice a lamb or a sheep at Eid al-Adha. One-third of the meat is given away to the poor. This is to remind Muslims of a sacrifice that Abraham made thousands of years ago. (Muslims regard Abraham as a prophet of God.) You can read the story in the Qur'an (Sura 37, verses 81–113) or in the Bible (Genesis Chapter 22, verses 1–19).

Below are three girls in Tunis dressed in their best Eid clothes. They are having their photograph taken. Look carefully at the carpets hung up behind them.

These are some Eid cards.

Below you can see a boy in Turkey selling the skins of the lambs after they have been sacrificed.

Two other important days in the Muslim year are:
(1) The beginning of each new year. It is not at the same time as the western new year. (See Chapter 12.)
(2) The birthday of Muhammad. On this day Muslims have a holiday. They meet in groups to tell the stories about the prophet's life and teaching.

Note You will need a Qur'an or a Bible.
1. (a) When is Eid al-Fitr? (b) When is Eid al-Adha?
2. How does the day of Eid begin?
3. What else do Muslims do at Eid al-Fitr?
4. Look closely at the second picture. Describe the clothes the men and boys are wearing. Can you think of a good reason for wearing baggy trousers?
5. (a) What is the custom at Eid al-Adha? (b) Look in the Qur'an or the Bible and write down what sacrifice Abraham was asked to make.
6. What can you see on the top carpet behind the three girls in Tunis?
7. Write down some of the things *you* do when you have a holiday for a big festival.
8. Design your own Eid card to send to a Muslim friend.

II Family life

A Muslim family includes grandparents, uncles and aunts and cousins. Often the members of this 'extended' family live together and may work together.
Muhammad left strict rules about Muslim family life.

BIRTH
All Muslim male babies must be circumcised. In this picture the doctor is saying a prayer with the parents before he circumcises the baby.
He will cut off the foreskin at the end of the penis.
It is also the custom to shave a new baby's head.

WOMEN
The Qur'an says that men should respect women and be good to them. Women must inherit a share of their parents' wealth.
Women in Muslim countries are expected to behave very differently from women in western countries.
Generally they do not mix freely with men.
All Muslim men and women should dress modestly.
Many Muslim women still hide their bodies and even their faces behind veils.

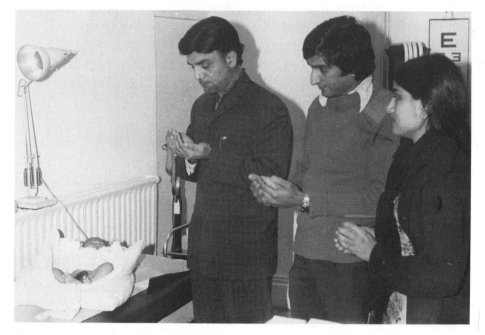

Muslims are often shocked when they come to western countries and see how some people dress. They believe that a woman should not wear clothes which show off her body. She should not 'tempt' men in this way. This is why even in this country many Muslim women cover their legs and arms and hair. This may make it difficult for girls to join in P.E. and swimming at school.

A Pakistani Muslim girl

— kameez

— shalwar

MARRIAGE
Many Muslim parents are very strict: their daughters may not go out to youth clubs and mix with boys. They believe that Muslim girls should keep themselves for marriage. Usually the parents look for suitable partners for their daughters and sons. Sometimes the young couple do not meet until the wedding day. More often these days, they are allowed more freedom in the choice.
The wedding does not have to be in a mosque, it can be in the bride's home. Usually the wedding is led by the local Imam. The bride and the groom are asked if they accept each other. They recite and sign a marriage contract. The bride is given a sum of money by the bridegroom's father. If they later divorce, that money remains hers.

Muhammad said that a Muslim man may have up to four wives, but he must treat them all in the same way. These days most Muslims have only one wife. If a man does marry again it is usually because his first wife cannot have a child.

OLD PEOPLE

When Muslim men and women become old they are not put into 'Old People's Homes'. Muslim families look after their grandparents. They respect them and turn to them for advice.

DEATH

The last words Muslims will say (if they can) are: 'There is only one God and Muhammad is his Prophet.' When someone dies, the body is wrapped in a white sheet after it has been washed. Prayers are said and the body is buried in a grave, the face turned towards Mecca. Many towns in Britain have graveyards for Muslims only. These graveyards are visited by Muslims who pray for the dead. They believe that there is a life after death. The Qur'an has a lot to say about heaven and hell. One sura says, 'Unto God we belong and unto God we shall return.'

Below: Musicians play at a wedding in Afghanistan

Above: A friend helps a Pakistani bride to get dressed for her wedding

Left: A funeral procession near Jerusalem

Above: A graveyard in Afghanistan

1. Describe what is happening in the photograph on p. 22.
2. How should Muslim men treat women?
3. Why are Muslims often shocked when they come to Britain?
4. Many Muslim girls are not allowed to go to youth clubs. Why?
5. Do you think parents should have any say in whom their children marry? Give reasons.
6. Describe a Muslim wedding ceremony.
7. What happens to old people?
8. (a) What happens to the body of a dead Muslim? (b) What do Muslims believe happens to people after death?
9. What would you like to happen to your body when you die?
10. Draw a Muslim girl to show what sort of clothes she might wear.

12 Language and dates

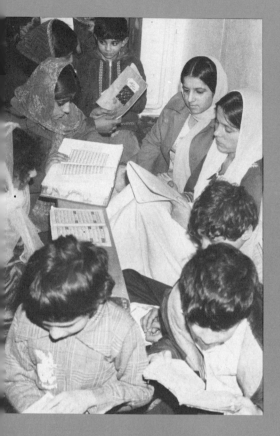

On p. 6 there is a photograph of a Qur'an. The writing is in Arabic, the language of the Arabs. The Arabs were the first Muslims, but now there are Muslims all over the world. Of course, Muslims speak the language of their own country, but many Muslim children also learn Arabic.

Arabic text of the Qur'an   What it says in Urdu   Explanation (in Urdu) of what it means

The children in the photograph on the left live in Birmingham. They have come to 'madrasah' after school to learn their own language and to study the Qur'an.

Look closely at the picture above. It shows the copy of the Qur'an that the children are reading. It is written in Arabic, but the writing underneath the shaded lines is what it means in Urdu. (Urdu is the main language spoken in Pakistan.) Both Arabic and Urdu are read from right to left.

Many mosques are beautifully decorated with patterns and script. The minaret on the left has verses from the Qur'an as part of its pattern. Can you see them? The picture of a ship, above, is made up of Arabic letters. It tells what Muslims believe about God. The word Allah has been coloured blue.